A Celtic Garden

by Philomena Durcan

Celtic Design Company, Sunnyvale, California.

Book Design by Colm Sweetman
Photography by Gillian Buckley and Colm Sweetman
Illustrations by Belinda Carroll
Editing by Elizabeth Feinler
Printed by Regent Printing Co., Hong Kong

First Edition

Library of Congress Catalog Card No.: 94-096818
Library of Congress Cataloging-in-Publication Data
        Durcan, Philomena
        A Celtic Garden / by Philomena Durcan

        1. Applique--Patterns.   2. Quilts--Celtic
        3. Patchwork--Patterns   4. Designs, Floral
        5. Quilting techniques--Bias Bar Applique
        6. Fabric art

ISBN 0-9631982-2-X (softcover)

Celtic Design Company
P.O. Box 2643
Sunnyvale, CA 94087

Contents

Foreword

A Celtic Garden is a continuation of my fascination with Celtic design. However, the inspiration for this book did not come from medieval manuscripts and Gaelic architecture like my other books. Rather it came from the gorgeous gardens of Ireland and Scotland, and the carpets of flowers strewn with breathtaking abandon across the Celtic countrysides.

Two years ago, after I had completed a three-day Celtic workshop at Audrey MacDougall's shop, Calico Threads, in Dunoon, Scotland, one of my students, Kay Cruden, invited me to go for a stroll with her through Benmore Botanical gardens which were close by. The sights were awe inspiring! I was greeted by a hillside of rhododendrons of all colors imaginable - white, pink, purple, and red highlighted against the many shades of green foliage backing them. There were paths that led us to intimate garden glens, where exotic flowers and shrubs had been encouraged to mingle here and there with the local plants to add excitement and pleasure to the view.

On looking back into the valley, we could see the mist mingled with morning light presenting an hauntingly beautiful sight. We could also see the majestic old stone house with its formal gardens and lawn, all carefully combed and manicured, and its special architectural features, like the old wrought iron gates that adorn the area around the house.

These views evoked many cherished memories of my childhood growing up in Ireland. Springtime was always a special time to admire the fields of daffodils and tulips beaded with morning dew. There were exquisite displays of cowslips (yellow primroses) that grew wild along the ditches. My sister Bride and I often picked bouquets of them for the May alter, although I must confess they did not all make it to the alter. We enjoyed sucking the nectar from these delicate beauties.

My family and I often visited the Botanic Gardens in Dublin. Here many of the displays were temperature-controlled, so there were exotic plants from many countries and climates to see. The lily pond was my special place of repose and serenity. We also visited many of the formal gardens around the Irish estates and castles. I remember them as places of beauty and inspiration.

On that particular day, as I gazed out at the elegance of Scotland, all of these old memories of Irish gardens flooded back through my mind and mingled with what was in front of me. I saw quilts in all directions, and I was off again on a new phase of Celtic design! I hope you, my readers and students, enjoy applying the designs as much as I enjoyed creating them for you, and that all your designs delight you.

Philomena Durcan.

Top: Benmore Botanical Garden

Left: Celtic Tulips, Philomena Durcan 1993, 30"x36"

4

Introduction

The colors and shapes of flowers are infinite and yet they are common and familiar to almost everyone. In that respect they are much like quilts. Flowers are the consummate token of love and friendship and suggest gentility and elegance with their fragrance and simplicity. Who has not marvelled at their variety and beauty and enjoyed their universal appeal! And who does not feel a pang of nostalgia remembering a gift of flowers from some yesteryear, or some special spot where flowers blanketed the ground with brilliant color. What a challenge to capture and hold even a tiny nuance of these impressions in applique!

Gillian Buckley

In preparing for this book, I researched a number of flower art forms from the past, particularly those derived from Celtic Art. Flowers have, of course, been a source of inspiration for all kinds of artists and crafts people for centuries. The flower can be found in every art form from ancient times to the present. In Asia the use of flowers in art is often stylized into design motifs or depicted in delicate brush paintings. In the Middle East flowers are an integral part of beautiful rug and mosaic designs, and in Europe they occur throughout illuminated manuscripts and intricate wall tapestries. Beginning in the 16th Century, European artists, particularly the Dutch, made flowers a common theme for their still-life paintings. In fact Pierre Joseph Redoute (1759-1840) was called the "Raphael of Flowers" and was a very prominent artist of his time whose work has endured. (Ref. 1)

Flower art continued to be a common theme among artists up through the Impressionists, then the Modernists. Van Gogh, Monet, Tiffany, O'Keefe and many others interpreted light, color, and composition through floral art. Today we are experiencing yet another romance with the flower in art and design, and people are again taking delight in using them to add comfort and warmth to their homes. Indeed, what can be more welcoming as a message of love and friendship in your home than a display of flowers. Flowers have always been offered with feeling and received with pleasure among friends and loved ones.

Flowers have been a perennial theme in fabric design and interior decorating as well as in painting and prints. They come into vogue again and again because they are so pleasing to both the spirit and the eye, and because they add drama and dimension to a room by softening the stark geometric lines of walls, ceilings and floors. In fabric art Elly Sienkiewicz epitomizes the use of flower motifs in her beautiful Baltimore Album Quilt designs (Refs. 2, 3, 4) also Nancy Pearson in her *Floral Appliques* (Ref. 5.) Laura Munson Reinstatler has emphasized leaves and foliage along with flowers in her book, *Botanical Wreaths* (Ref. 6.) Jeana Kimball has also developed lovely flower designs for quilters. (Ref. 7.)

Right: Rosemary Kurtz 1994, 14"x14" Rosemary adapted Philomena's Tulip design and was awarded a Blue Ribbon at her local Quilt Show

Right page: *Through the Garden Gate,* Philomena Durcan 1994, 42"x66" Quilted by Rosemary Kurtz

I myself explored many possible ways to develop flower designs that captured the essence of the Celtic gardens of Ireland and Scotland. Finally I decided to keep the flower patterns themselves simple, and let bias layering and use of color and fabric add depth, texture, and richness to the

finished designs. In my mind's eye I imagined seeing the flowers through rustic iron gates or through old Irish garden walls, so I combined the Celtic interlace patterns from my first book, *Celtic Quilt Designs* (Ref. 8) with the floral designs included here to achieve this effect. The illustrations throughout the book will give you an idea of what I mean. You might want to look at them to get ideas or to learn how to create a similar effect in your own design. The flower patterns may be used as color applique, as background quilt designs, or as a mixture of both. Varying the types of borders and block sashing will also create different effects. Experiment until you get an effect you like.

The bulk of the book is made up of the Celtic Floral Designs themselves. There are thirteen different designs in all with complete cutting and appliqueing instructions, as well as a pull-out design for the *Through the Garden Gate* wall hanging. You will note that each design piece is numbered and directional arrows have been added to assist you with laying down the bias trim. You are also told how many of each piece to cut. Each design is sized for a typical 16" block; however, they can be scaled up or down using a pantograph tracing tool available from most art stores.

All the tools you will need are described and step-by-step instructions are given for assembling the block and appliqueing the bias trim using the Celtic Design Company bias-bar technique. This technique greatly simplifies the art of applique. It is very effective for adding a dramatic, 3-dimensional effect to your work, and yet is easy enough for beginners to use.

The sections on Color and Design and Fabric discuss the process of choosing fabrics and colors to create special floral effects. Here I have tried to share with you how I choose fabric and color to follow the form and texture of the flowers. Careful selection of color and fabric will make the difference between a finished piece that appears to be flat and inanimate and one that has rich texture and seems to come alive.

The section on Finishing Techniques gives you ideas about assembling and quilting your finished piece such as how to arrange and separate the blocks or what kinds of borders are pleasing. This book, being a design book, does not give you specific detail on how to assemble and quilt; however, it references excellent books that cover these instructions in detail. Illustrations of various types of finished pieces are included throughout the book to suggest ideas and approaches for your own work, and to show you the fragile splendor of the gardens of Ireland and Scotland which were and are such an integral part of my Celtic heritage.

Above: *Through the Garden Wall,* Philomena Durcan 1994 52"x52"

Right page: Lily, Daffodil, Rose, Hibiscus, Primrose and Poppy, all are 16" blocks using a variety of hand-dyed and commercial fabrics.

8

Designing your Block

COLOR AND DESIGN

The color and fabric design approach I have used is one of "painting" with fabric. Think of each of your blocks as a fabric "still life" or a series of related "still-lifes" with a unifying theme. The essence of the technique is to select fabric colors, designs, tones, and patterns that, when incorporated into the flower applique, suggest the color and texture of the flower as it exists in nature. Using this technique the petals of an individual flower are more apt to be composed of a series of analogous colors, such as pink through red to fuschia; or different values of the same color, such as several values of the same shade of blue, rather than be made up of contrasting complementary colors, such as red and green. Use the same color fabric, an analogous color, or lighter or darker color value, rather than a contrasting color for the bias trim. This will add depth and movement to the flower design rather than make it look "outlined." Contrast can be added by using complementary colors for the block background or by using complementary colors for the flower designs in alternating blocks.

To get started consider the area where you want to use the piece you are creating. Choose colors that will fit in with the decor of the room it will be in, and a scale that is suitable for the place in which it will be displayed. The flower designs work well on quilts, wall hangings, pillow covers, and clothing. Decide whether you want your piece to be predominantly warm colors (reds, yellows, oranges, and pinks) or cool colors (blues, greens, and violets). Will the background be light or dark? To create the illusion of looking through an iron gate or stone wall make the "gate" applique darker, then go from dark toward a light background. To create the illusion of seeing flowers through a lattice, reverse this process. Diana Leone has written an interesting book, *Attic Windows* (Ref. 9) which may also give you some ideas along these lines. She has taken a more contemporary approach.

It is a good idea to make several sketches of your finished piece until you find something that pleases you in scale and design. If you are making several blocks, be sure to figure in any block sashing and borders in estimating the overall size. Once you have the basic concept of the piece in mind, you can begin selecting fabric and colors to carry out the theme.

Top: The Pansy, Rosella Keller, 1994 18"x18" A class project.

Bottom: A combination of hand-dyed and commercial fabrics that blend well together

Right page: A small sample of the vast variety of commercial fabrics available for floral applique.

FABRIC

The fabric choices today are fabulous! A visit to your local quilt store will introduce you to a large selection. Fabrics from the big manufacturers, such as EZ International's Chapel House Division and Hoffman International Fabrics are excellent. I have also used wonderful fabrics from several smaller specialty suppliers, such as Island Fibers, Skydyes, and Shades, Inc. If you are new to fabric art, you might consider buying several "fat quarters" of fabric of various colors and patterns from different manufacturers and experiment with them. Most quilt stores have a large selection of "fat quarters" available.

You must train your eye to choose the right fabric "paint." Try using large floral prints that have color and activity similar to the flowers you have chosen. You can often cut petals from one portion and leaves from another portion of these large prints. Mottled fabrics in light and dark tones of the same color are wonderful to work with, as are monotone or variegated tie-dyed fabrics. The mottled and tie-dyed fabrics are excellent for flowers because they add depth and movement. You will find that bias made from the same fabric as the straight-cut flower petals will have quite a different look because it is cut on the diagonal. It will add interest and dimension rather than stark contrast.

Study the flowers in nature, if you can, or study cut blooms in flower shops or flower arrangements. Then look for patterns in fabric that mimic the patterns in flowers in their natural state. For instance, spotted fabric might work for the petals of day lilies with contrasting anthers; roses might start with darker shades in the center and lighter shades at the edges; pansies might have dark petals and light petals on the same bloom; tulips might be striped, and daffodils and hibiscus could have faint striations on their petals. This is where the "painting" and your artistic creativity come in. Do not try to simply copy nature; rather interpret it with your own genius and ingenuity.

I recommend 100% cotton fabric for quilt making. It feels good and is easy to care for. A 50/50 cotton-polyester combination can be used for the petals and leaves, but a lightweight 100% cotton is highly recommended for the bias.

Top: The Iris Garden and an Iris block in progress

Bottom: A variety Of hand-dyed fabrics.

Right page: Celtic Peony Rose, Philomena Durcan (© 1990) Featuring analogous & complementary color combinations (pattern not included)

Constructing your Block

CHECKLIST OF STEPS

Below is a checklist of the 10 basic steps you will perform to complete your applique project. They are presented in the order in which the tasks will be performed, and will give you a comprehensive overview of what is involved.

Step 1.   Collect together all the tools and supplies listed below.

Step 2.   Trace the complete version of the chosen flower design pattern from the pattern in the book onto 11" x 17" tracing vellum. If you are using several of the flower designs, repeat the process for each flower design.

Step 3.   Trace the chosen designs onto the background fabric.

Step 4.   Make paper templates for cutting out the individual applique pieces that make up the complete design.

Step 5.   Cut out the fabric pieces for each flower and baste them onto the traced design on your background block.

Step 6.   Make the bias trim.

Step 7.   Applique the bias trim on top of each flower design.

Step 8.   Assemble the appliqued blocks (if your project is composed of multiple blocks.)

Step 9.   Trace your background quilting design onto the front of the quilt (Celtic Design Company stencils can be used to help with this.)

Step 10.   Add the batting and backing; then quilt the final work in the usual manner.

TOOLS

Applique quilting is fine work, and it requires fine tools. It is important to have the right tools and supplies to do the job. Here is a list of items you will need to get started.

- Thread to match your fabrics
- Quilting needles, #10 or #12. John James #12 Sharps and Piecemakers #12 applique needles are both excellent and highly recommended.
- A thimble (Your fingers will thank you!)
- Three pairs of scissors, one to cut paper, one to cut fabric, and one for close trimming.
- An iron and ironing board.
- A rotary cutter and cutting board for cutting bias. (Available from most quilt shops.)
- A see-through Omnigrid 6" x 24" plastic ruler that measures down to 1/8".
- A corkboard, 18" x 24" (preferred) or other foam core pinboard.
- A tracing paper pad, 18" x 24".
- A washable Ultimate Marking Pencil for Quilters or #3 hard lead pencil.
- A fine black marking pen.
- A 1/8" Celtic Design Company metal Bias Bar for making bias to outline the floral patterns; 3/16", 1/4", 3/8", 1/2", 5/8", and 3/4" metal Bias Bars for embellishment or special effects, depending upon your design.
- A color wheel.
- A light box or table (optional.)

Right Page:
Top Left: Aoife, A Celtic Spiral Wall Hanging. Pat Peters, Bishop, CA. This wall hanging was made for The Calico Quilters 1994 Fabric Challenge Contest where it took first place. It is one of the designs from my book, *Celtic Spirals.*

Top Right: Tulip Stencil, 17"x17" (available in stencil only)

Bottom Left: Celtic Sampler, Pat Peters, Bishop, CA. 1994 68"x92". This Quilt won Best of Show at the 1994 Eastern Sierra Tri-County Fair 1994. These are some of the designs from my book, *Celtic Quilt Designs.*

Bottom Right: Roisin, Philomena Durcan 1993 35"x35" One of the designs from my book, *Celtic Spirals.*

A. Tracing the whole design on to 11"x17" vellum. Squaring up the 17"x17" block of fabric, and centering it.

B. Tracing the design onto background block.

C. Cutting out the cut-outs.

D. Basting the Daffodils to background block.

E. Laying the bias along the petal using blind applique stitch.

F. Mitering the corner at point of petal.

G. Tucking in the bias.

H. Appliqueing the next petal.

TRACING SELECTED DESIGNS ONTO BACKGROUND FABRIC

Select the flower patterns you wish to trace. We will use the Daffodil pattern on page 34 as an example for this discussion. The Daffodil flower itself is 13" long and 10" wide and is scaled to fit on a 16" finished block. Mark the center of a 17" square piece of tracing paper, then place it over the complete Daffodil design, and trace around it with the black marking pen. Be sure to match the center of the tracing paper with the center of the pattern as indicated by the crossed center markings on the pattern.

Now fold a block of 17" x 17" background fabric in half and then in half again. Pin or pinch the folded point of fabric that marks the center of the background block. Place the background fabric on top of the pattern to be traced, being careful to match the center markings on the pattern to the center of the background block. Note: Be careful to place the design on the vertical straight of the background fabric. Anchor the two layers with pins or tape so that they will not slip. Then trace the pattern onto the fabric using the Ultimate Marking Pencil or a #3 hard pencil.

If the background fabric is dark or opaque, the pattern may be difficult to trace. If so, try using a light box or table, or taping both the pattern and the fabric to a window with light coming through from behind. This will make the pattern lines easier to see through the fabric.

Repeat this process for each flower design you will be using.

MAKING APPLIQUE CUT-OUT TEMPLATES

Once you have traced your chosen design onto the background block, you are then ready to cut out the fabric pieces that will be appliqued to it. We will refer to these pieces as "cut outs" or "applique pieces" for convenience.

Use good quality tracing or drafting paper for tracing your cut-out templates from the ones in the book. The patterns in the book are numbered to distinguish one piece from another. Be sure to write these numbers on the traced copies, so that you do not have to keep referring back to the book to check which piece is which. Also, trace the dotted lines that indicate the seam allowances for the pieces that tuck under. Trace any other markings that appear on the originals onto your copies.

CUTTING OUT THE APPLIQUE PIECES

Note that each pattern piece is clearly marked as to how many of that particular pattern piece should be cut. If duplicate pattern pieces are indicated and you wish them to be similar, cut them as follows: Place two layers of fabric together both with **right sides facing up**, and with pattern and straight of fabric going in the same direction. Lay the template on the fabric, and pin it down. Then cut both pieces at once. The important thing to remember is that both pieces of fabric should have their right sides facing up.

Because you will be using your fabric to create a floral "still life," you may wish to vary duplicate pieces to fit the color and contour of your design. Also, you may choose to cut each piece and try it as you go, somewhat like an artist would add and modify color until the right effect is achieved. This style of applique does not lend itself to cutting out the design pieces in "cooky cutter" fashion; instead it tends to be a trial-and-error process to achieve the most pleasing colors and patterns and the best fabric representation of the flower.

Don't be in a hurry. Use trial and error. Pin pattern pieces, piece-by-piece, onto the design traced onto your background block; then hang the resulting block on the wall and back away from it. Does the combination of the color and the fabric pattern give you the effect you are after? If not, try other combinations until you like what you see before you stitch it down. This is the essence of "painting" with fabrics.

BASTING THE APPLIQUE PIECES TO THE BACKGROUND BLOCKS

Now that you have cut your applique pattern pieces and like the way they fit into your overall design, you are ready to baste them to the background block. Lay your background block flat on the corkboard. Now begin laying down the cut-out pieces in numerical order onto the background block, matching them to the design you have traced onto the background block. You will note that the lower-numbered pieces are the ones that have seam allowances (indicated by the dotted lines.) Continue laying down the pieces and pinning them in place until the pattern is completed. Note that the pieces without seam allowances overlap the pieces that have the seam allowances. Once you have assembled and pinned down all the pattern pieces in the right sequence, then baste all the applique pieces to the background block. It is very important to baste the pieces that overlap with small stitches, so that the pieces stay in place and do not slip or separate.

MAKING THE BIAS

Now you are ready to make the bias stripping. The bias is appliqued over the raw edge of the pattern pieces you have just basted to your background fabric. It serves as a finish for the raw edges. The bias stripping is what adds depth or contrast to the block and is itself an important part of the overall design. When "painting" with fabric, try using the same fabric you used for the cut-out applique pieces to make the bias stripping. Or choose a close analogous color rather than a contrasting color. You might think this would create a dull flower or leaf with little contrast. Actually it adds depth and texture to your piece; whereas bias stripping that is a contrasting color tends to give the finished flower an unnatural "outlined" look.

SIZE	FABRIC
16" quilt block -	1/2 to 2/3 yard of fabric
52"x52" sampler -	2 1/2 yards of fabric
40"x66" wall hanging -	5 1/2 yards of fabric

Scale the bias trim to the pattern you have chosen. One-eighth inch bias stripping is the size recommended for outlining the Celtic Floral Designs. Larger bias strips, such as the 1/2", 5/8", and 3/4" can be used to embellish blocks or wall hangings. These larger sizes of bias trim were used to obtain the "wrought-iron gate" effect as shown in the photograph on the cover. Bias bars for all the sizes mentioned here are available from Celtic Design Co., or from your local quilt shop.

The amount of bias needed is largely dependent upon the intricacy of the design. In the inset box we have given the amount of fabric needed for a typical 16" block and a 40" x 66" wall hanging. Because you will be using the "painting with fabric" technique, these numbers are only rough guidelines. Note that you do not need long pieces of bias to outline the flower and leaf parts. Most pieces are fairly short and the ends will be tucked in. Again, using the "painting with fabric" technique, you may wish to vary the bias slightly from one place to another in the design depending upon the amount of contrast you need. Save all your scraps. What does not get used for bias may make the next petal or leaf and vice versa.

Make ⅛" bias stripping as follows:

1 If your fabric is 36" wide, measure off a 36" square of fabric. This will give you a block of fabric 36" x 36". Smooth the fabric, and then fold it in half diagonally to form two triangles of fabric back-to-back with a fold along the upper edge. If your fabric is 44" wide, first cut the fabric carefully down the center into two 22" widths. Measure 22" in length on the square of fabric to produce a block of fabric 22" x 22". Again fold the fabric square in half diagonally to form two triangles of fabric back-to-back with the fold along the upper edge. Press the fabric very lightly along the fold with a hot iron.

Note: It is very important that the bias be cut along the diagonal fold of a true square of fabric. This will give you "true" bias. Fabric cut any other way will not produce "true" bias, which means it will not have the necessary stretching properties to follow the curves of your pattern and will buckle and pucker.

2 Using a see-through ruler, measure ¾" away from the fold.

3 Cut with the rotary cutter along the edge of the ruler to make a bias strip. Measure down another ¾" and cut the next bias strip, and so forth until all the fabric has been cut into bias.

4 Fold each strip of bias with the right facing sides out, and machine sew down the center of the folded fabric. Trim the raw edges back to the seam. You now have a tube of fabric.

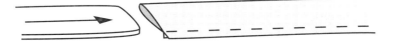

Note: There is no need to sew the strips of bias together to make one long piece of bias because the ends of the bias tuck under. Use the longer pieces of bias for the biggest edges and the shorter pieces for the smaller edges.

5 Now insert a ⅛" Bias Bar into each tube, rolling the seam to the center of a flat side of the metal bar.

6 With the Bias Bar still inserted, steam press the tube with the seam down the center and with both seam edges facing to one side. Push the bar forward through the tube until the entire strip is pressed. You should now have a strip of bias ⅛" wide with the seam down the center of the backside ready to applique to your basted pattern.

TRUE BIAS

ADDING BIAS TO THE APPLIQUED DESIGN

Please note that the sequence in which the bias is added is particularly important because there will be many raw bias ends to hide by tucking them in under the piece of bias that goes over their top. If you do not lay down the bias in the right sequence, there will be nowhere to tuck in these ends. If you do lay the bias down in the proper sequence, most of the ends will tuck in nicely.

Before you begin adding bias trim look at the Daffodil pattern on page 36. Note the small insets on this page marked "A" and "B." These are sequence diagrams. Now note the bold line on the sequence diagram that begins with an open dot, ends with a black or closed dot, and has directional arrows in between. This bold line indicates where to start laying down the bias and where to end.

① Lay the bias along the contour of the design. Add bias to the applique pieces in their numerical order, unless a special sequence is indicated in the margin of the pattern. Where such a sequence is given begin at the spot on the diagram indicated by the small open circle, lay down the bias in the direction indicated by the arrows, and end the piece of bias at the spot indicated by the small black circle. **Sew down the inside curve first. Do NOT sew down the outside edge yet.** Leave a 1/8" tail of bias for tucking under in each case.

② At the places where the bias changes direction abruptly, miter the point at which the direction changes by placing a pin through the bias at that point and folding the bias over to face in the new direction. Finger press the bias in place, needle in the surplus, and stitch it down using a blind applique stitch.

③ As you applique make sure that the raw seam on the bias is flaring outward on an outward curve. Sew down the inside curve first. Do NOT sew down the outside edges (particularly on the part indicated by a bold line on the sequence diagram) until you have tucked in all the ends leading up to it. Only then sew the outside edges over the tucked-in ends.

④ On some designs, such as the Daffodil, many stems and leaves terminate at the bottom of the design leaving several raw ends exposed. Use a single piece of bias to cover all of these raw ends. Then use your needle to tuck in the ends of this overlaying piece of bias and stitch down the ends to finish.

⑤ Continue in this fashion until the design is completed and all raw ends are tucked in.

⑥ Proceed in the same manner to the next block until all the blocks are appliqued.

Although the bias strip makes a lovely finish and adds a three-dimensional depth to your work, it is very difficult to make in widths less than 1/8". Also, on the flower designs, depending on the scale, there may be small pieces of the design that are too small to outline with bias. For this reason small pieces, such as centers and stamens, are usually finished by traditional applique methods without the bias.

Finishing Techniques

The exact details of assembly and finishing are beyond the scope of this book. A number of how-to books are listed in the Bibliography that are useful for learning some of the tried and true methods. (Refs. 10,11,12,13 and 14) Also, check your local schools and quilt shops for classes, or join a local quilting club in your area.

The pull-out pattern for *Through the Garden Gate* can be used to make the 40" x 66" wall hanging illustrated on the front of the book. Large bias trim was used (3/4" bias for the diamond and 1/2" bias for the circles) with the floral designs to give the effect of looking through a wrought-iron gate. The "wrought-iron" effect comes from using dark bias embellishment against a light background. A lattice effect can be achieved by using light bias embellishment over a dark background with the flowers showing through.

The larger bias can also be used to frame the blocks or as border trim for larger pieces such as quilts. The floral designs blend beautifully with simple Celtic interlace borders or with swag or leaf borders. Use your imagination! Several diagrams have been included on pages 22 through 25 to provide ideas for layouts. The Celtic Floral Designs can be inserted into these layouts. The flower designs make beautiful quilting patterns as well as applique designs. Quilted flowers can be used to embellish blocks or background areas that do not have an appliqued design in them. Colored and background blocks can be alternated and separated by sashing in various ways to make interesting combinations. Celtic interlace patterns can also be used for quilting or as framing to set off the flowers. Stencils of these are available from Celtic Design Co. or your local quilt store. Stencils are handy for tracing repeated patterns onto an assembled piece as a guide for quilting. For example, the wall hanging shown on page 15, Top Right, was bordered on the four corners by using the Celtic Design Company stencil, PD24.

We hope we have given you some ideas and examples for making Celtic Floral Design appliques. The flower patterns can, of course, be worked into a layout designed by you to create your own unique design, and they can be combined with other styles of applique layouts in which flowers occur. Enjoy both the doing and the viewing wherever you use them!

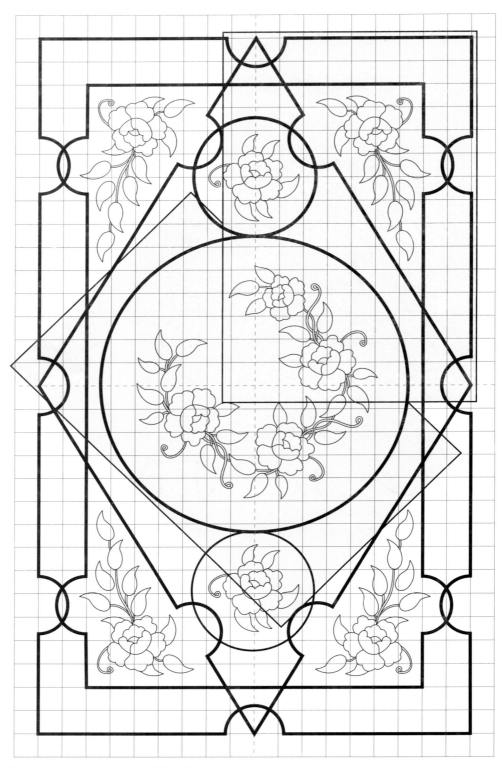

Through the Garden Gate grid, 1/4" = 2"
Poster tamplate area is indicated by shading

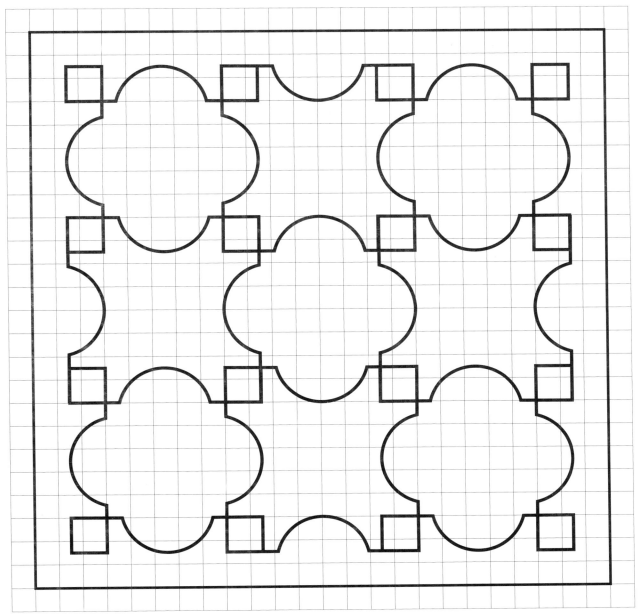

Through the Garden Wall grid, 1/4" = 2". Through the Garden Wall Samples.
This piece is appliqued by tracing designs on to a solid piece of background fabric. It is not assembled from blocks.

Poppy sampler

Mixed Flowers sampler

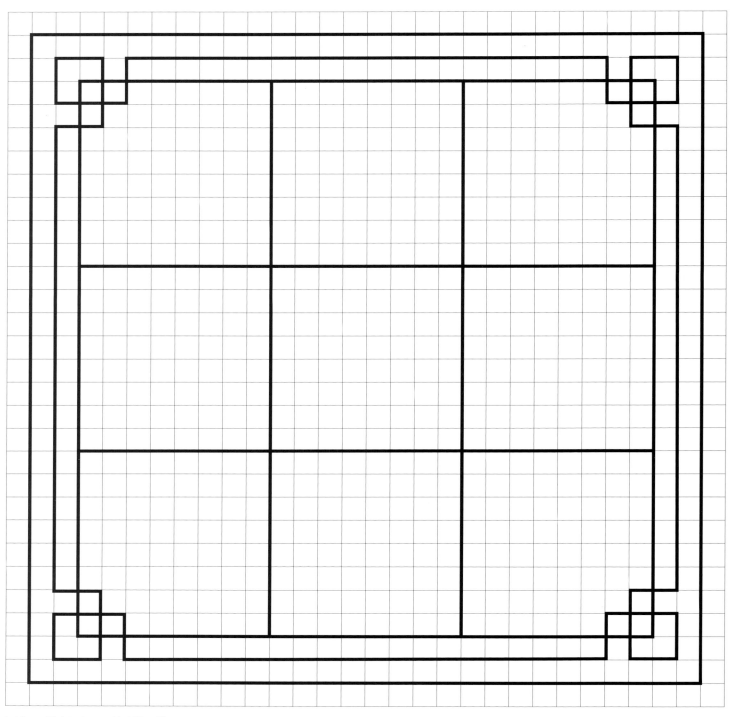

Lattice with Interlace grid, 1/4" = 2"
This is assembled from nine or more 16" blocks with Celtic Interlace trim.

Celtic Tulip grid, 1/4" = 2"

Mixed Flowers Sampler

Iris Sampler

Anemone

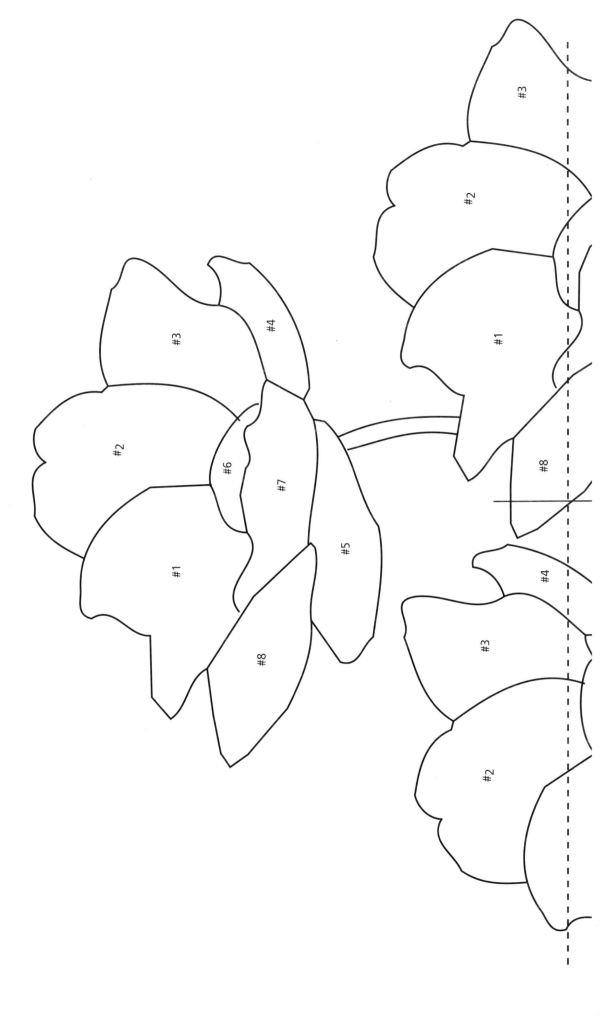

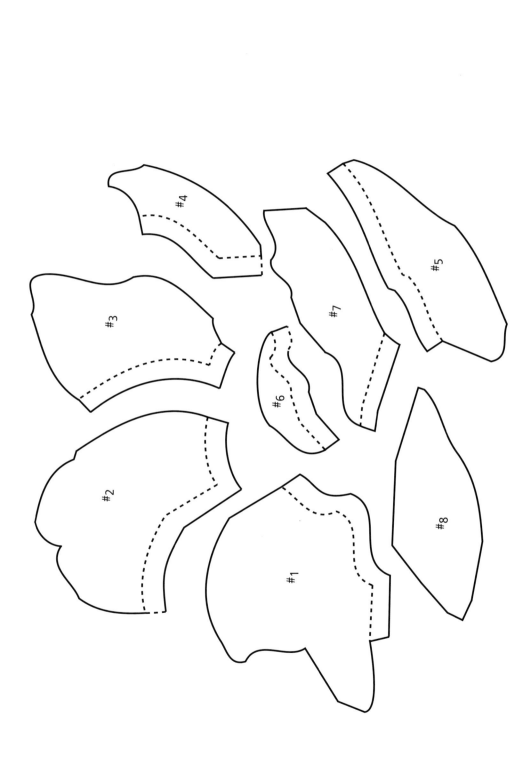

Bias Sequence Diagram

Begin by stitching a continuous strip of bias around the edges indicated by dark lines. Start at the open circle, follow the directional arrows, and stop at the closed circle. Stitch inside edge only. Add rest of bias. Tuck in raw edges. Finish stitching outside edges. See page 20 for details.

A

B

#5L

Clematis

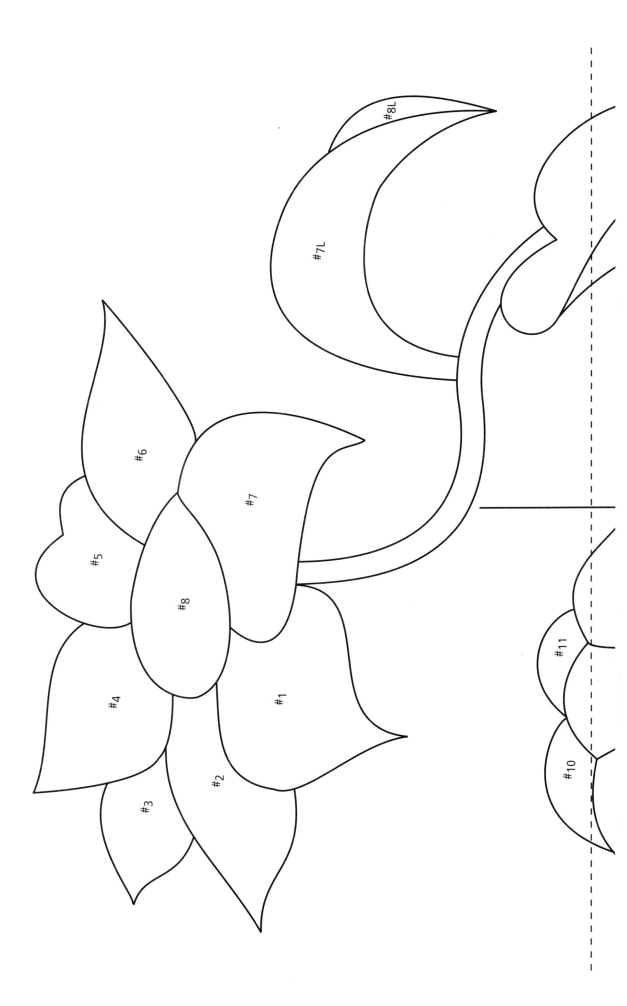

#8L

#7L

#6

#5

#7

#8

#4

#1

#11

#10

#3

#2

#6L

#5L

#3L

#4L

#2L

#1L

#12

#13

#15

#14

#9

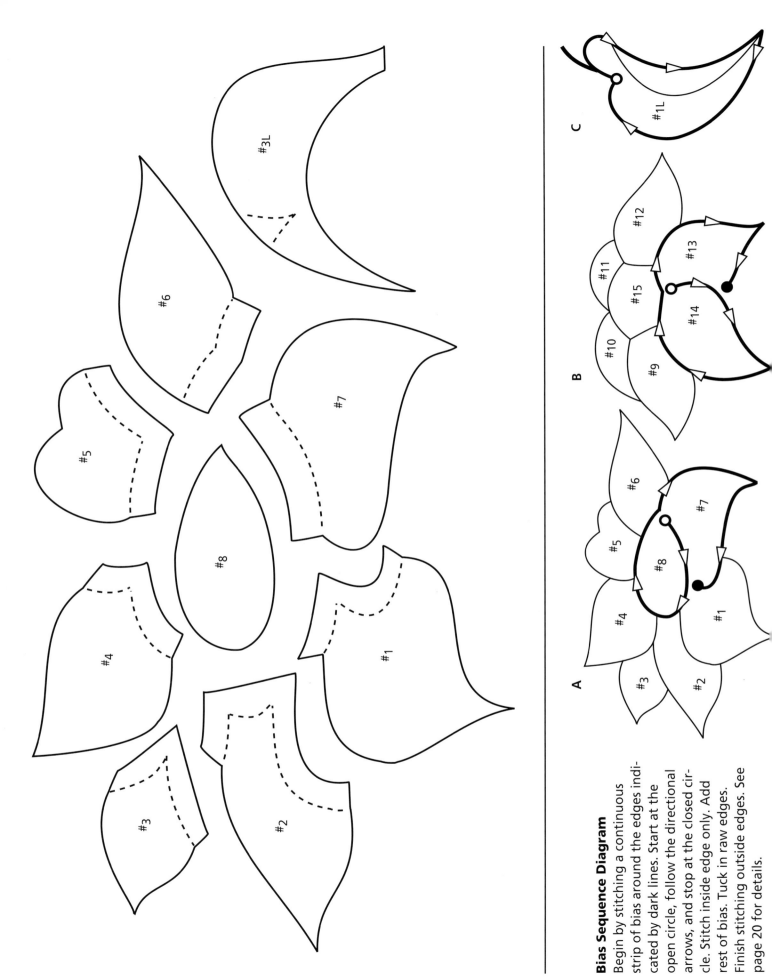

#3L

#6

#5

#7

#8

#4

#1

#3

#2

A

#3
#5
#4
#6
#8
#7
#1
#2

B

#11
#12
#10
#15
#13
#9
#14

C

#1L

Bias Sequence Diagram

Begin by stitching a continuous strip of bias around the edges indicated by dark lines. Start at the open circle, follow the directional arrows, and stop at the closed circle. Stitch inside edge only. Add rest of bias. Tuck in raw edges. Finish stitching outside edges. See page 20 for details.

Daffodils

#16

#17

#6L

#5L

#2L

#4L

#1L

#3L

#2L

#1L

#4L

#5L

#3L

#6L

Bias Sequence Diagram

Begin by stitching a continuous strip of bias around the edges indicated by dark lines. Start at the open circle, follow the directional arrows, and stop at the closed circle. Stitch inside edge only. Add rest of bias. Tuck in raw edges. Finish stitching outside edges. See page 20 for details.

A

B

C

#18

#16

#17

#1

#2

#3

#4

#6

#9

#10

#11

#12

#13

#14

#8

Hibiscus

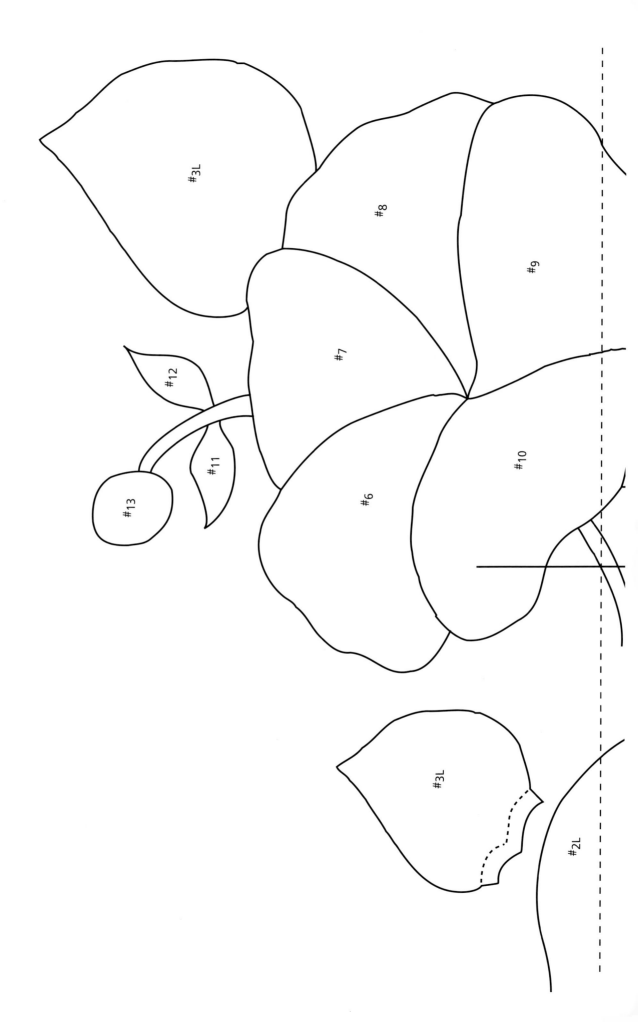

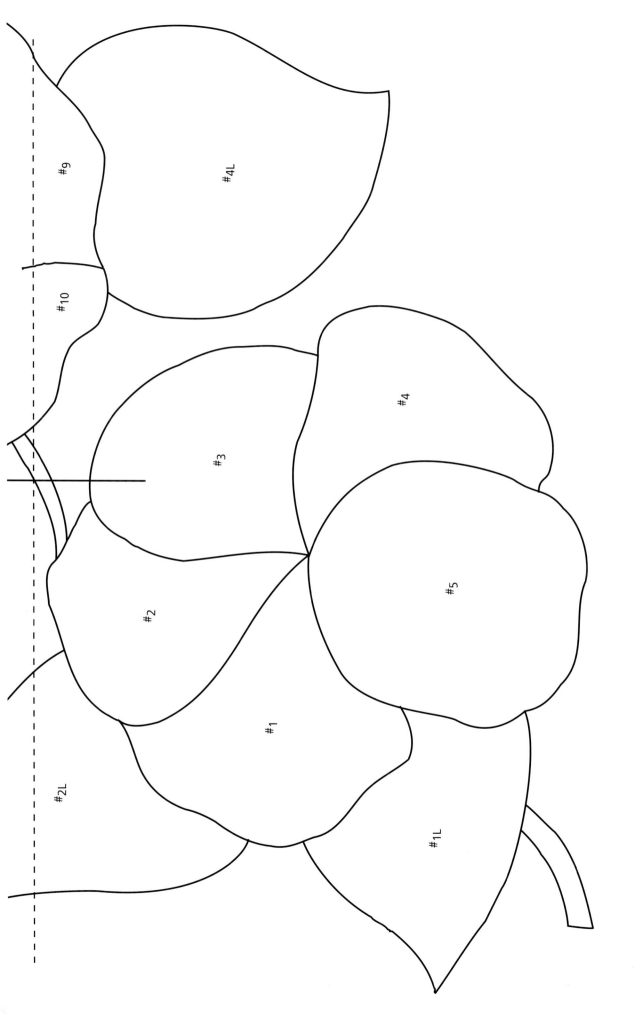

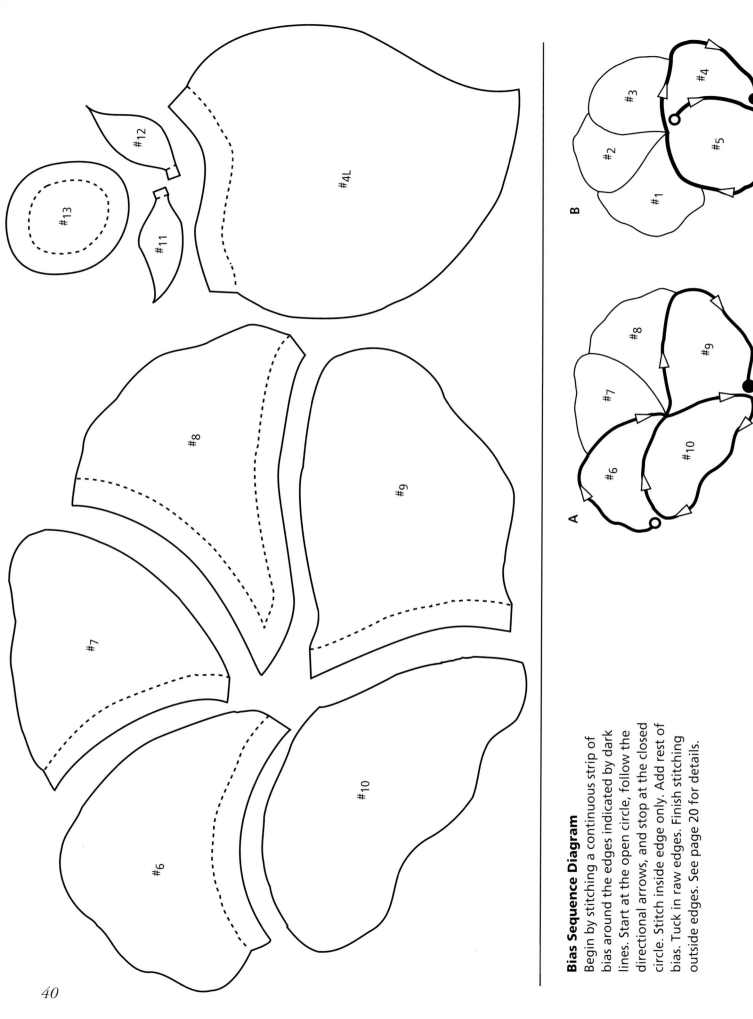

Bias Sequence Diagram

Begin by stitching a continuous strip of bias around the edges indicated by dark lines. Start at the open circle, follow the directional arrows, and stop at the closed circle. Stitch inside edge only. Add rest of bias. Tuck in raw edges. Finish stitching outside edges. See page 20 for details.

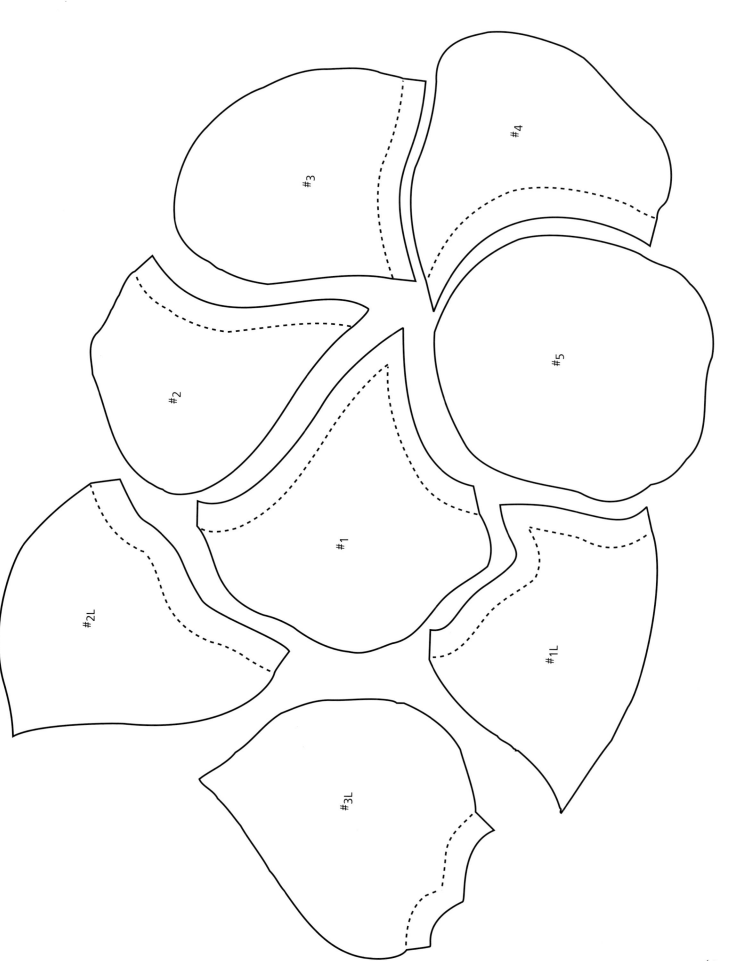

Iris

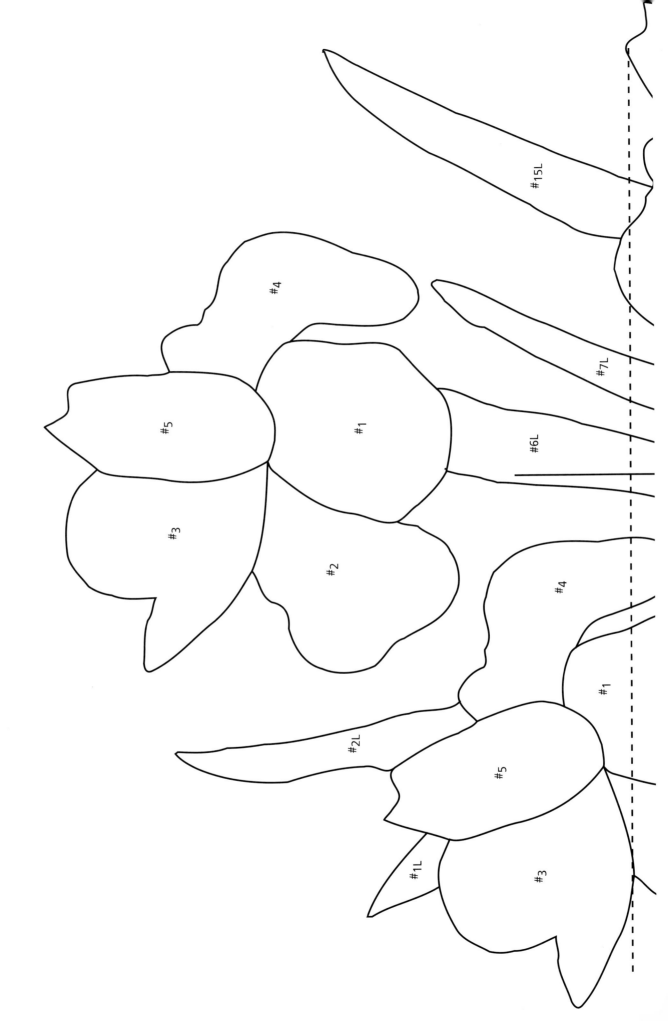

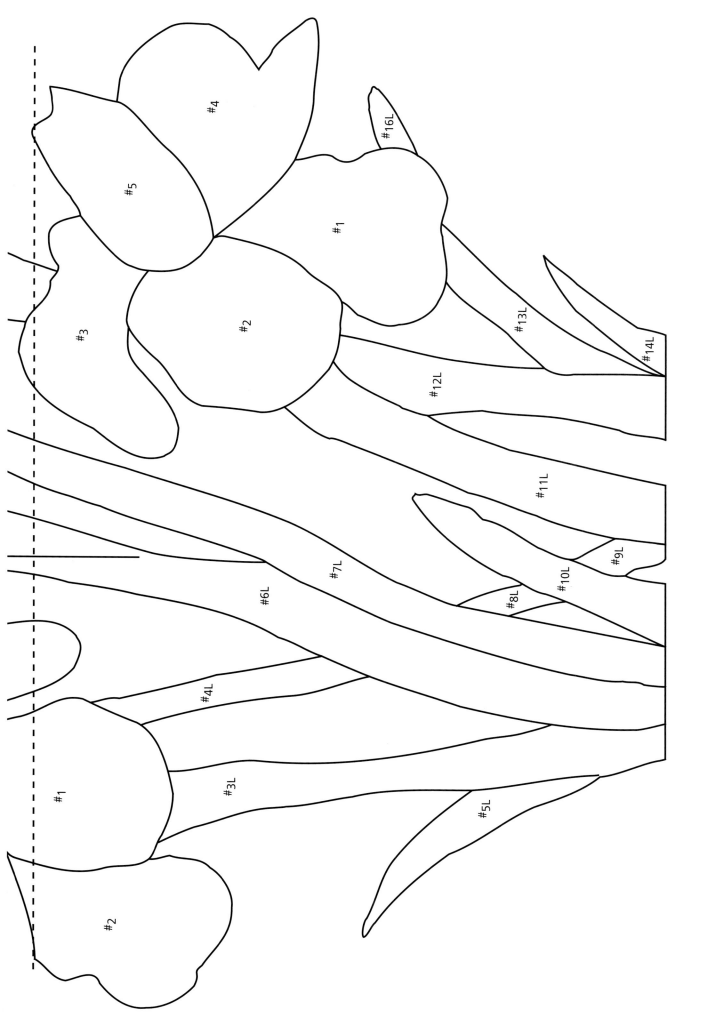

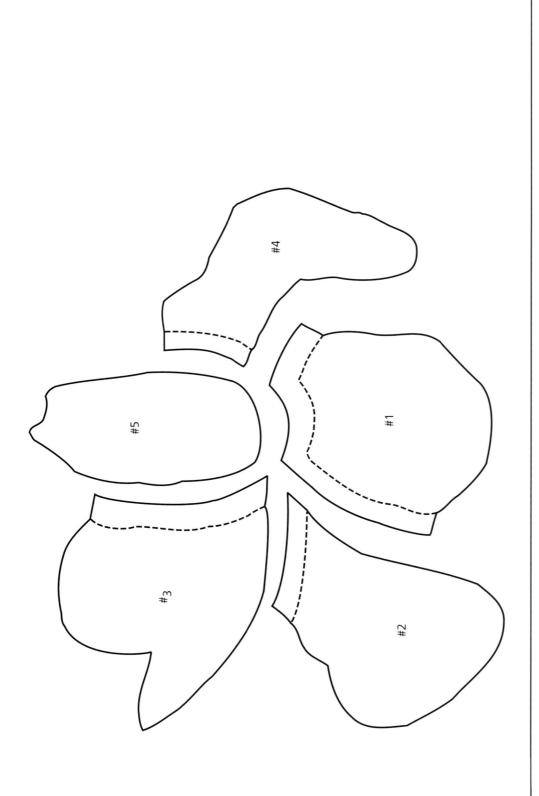

Bias Sequence Diagram

Begin by stitching a continuous strip of bias around the edges indicated by dark lines. Start at the open circle, follow the directional arrows, and stop at the closed circle. Stitch inside edge only. Add rest of bias. Tuck in raw edges. Finish stitching outside edges. See page 20 for details.

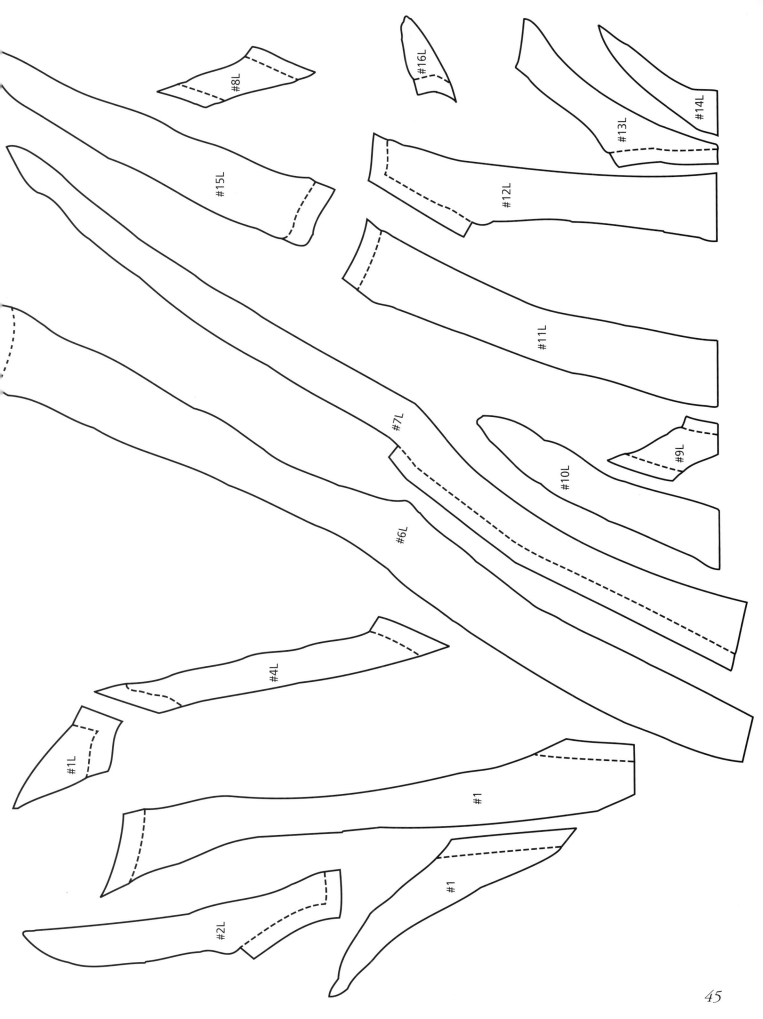

45

Lily

#15

#12

#13

#4L

#3L

#1L

#6L

#5L

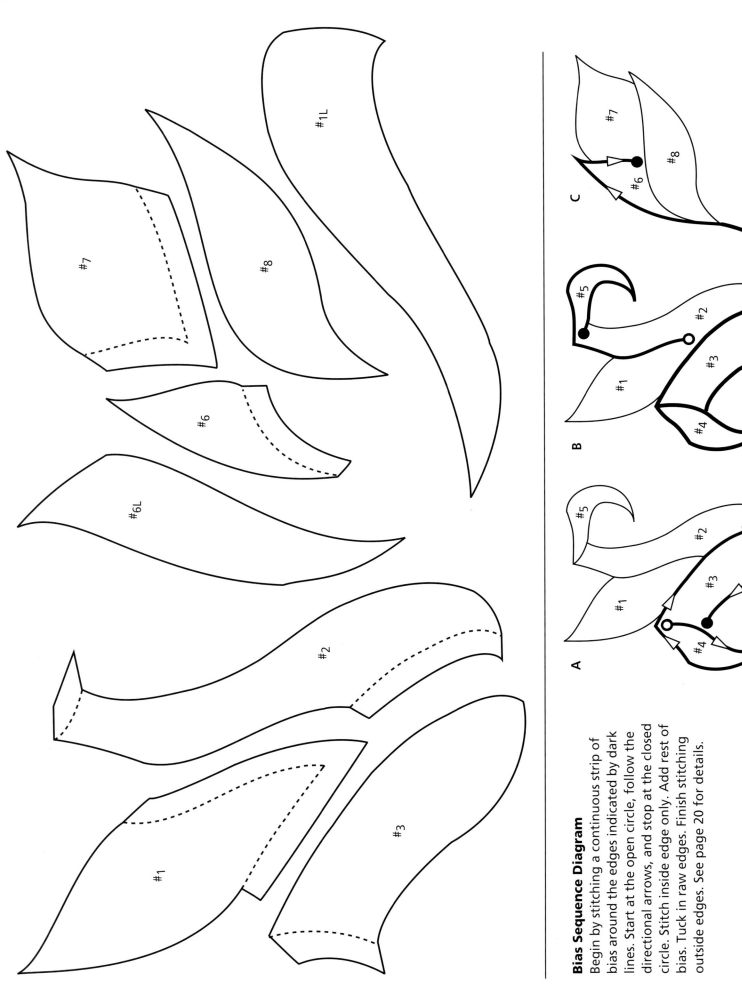

Bias Sequence Diagram

Begin by stitching a continuous strip of bias around the edges indicated by dark lines. Start at the open circle, follow the directional arrows, and stop at the closed circle. Stitch inside edge only. Add rest of bias. Tuck in raw edges. Finish stitching outside edges. See page 20 for details.

49

Pansy

#1

#2

#5

#3

#4

#6

#7

#5

#8

#9

#2L

#2

#5

#1

#4

#3

#3

#7

#6

#5

50

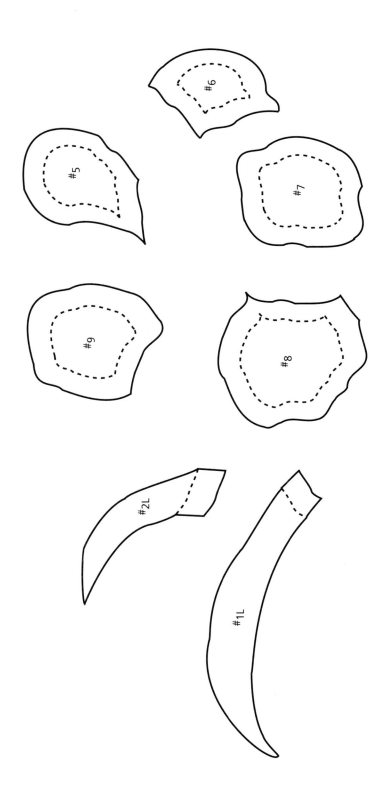

#6

#5

#7

#9

#8

#2L

#1L

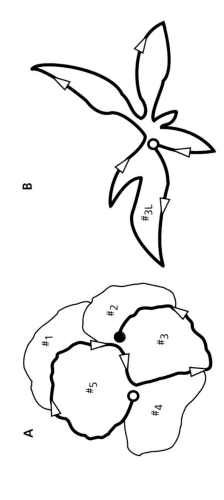

B

#3L

A

#1

#2

#3

#5

#4

Bias Sequence Diagram

Begin by stitching a continuous strip of bias around the edges indicated by dark lines. Start at the open circle, follow the directional arrows, and stop at the closed circle. Stitch inside edge only. Add rest of bias. Tuck in raw edges. Finish stitching outside edges. See page 20 for details.

Poppy

#2L

#7

#9

#10

#8

#6

#2

#11

#1

#13

#4

#5

#14

#3

#1L

54

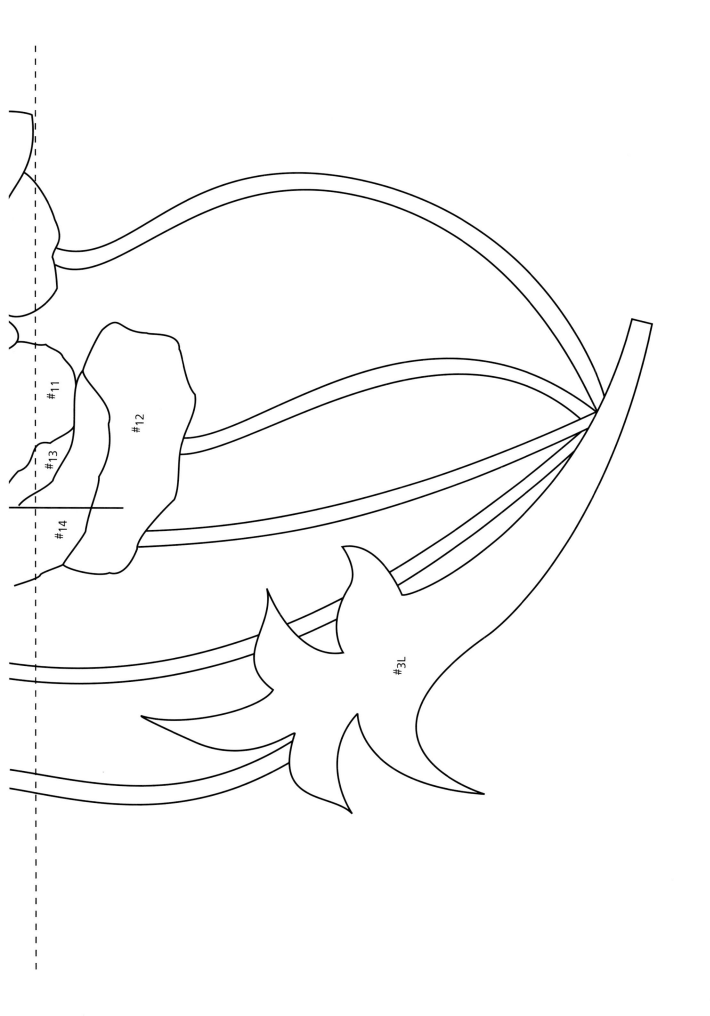

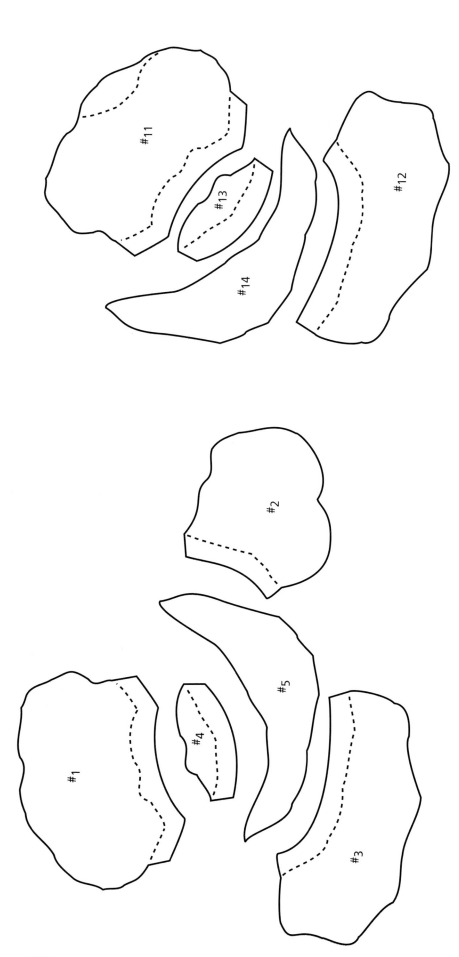

#11

#13

#14

#12

#2

#5

#4

#1

#3

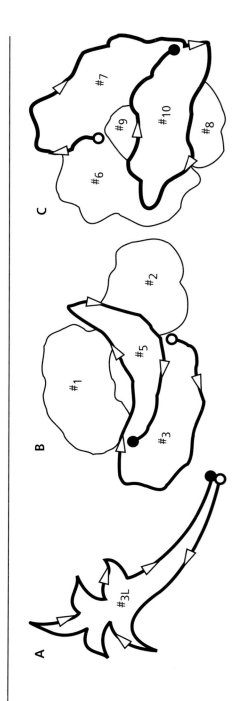

A

#3L

B

#1

#5

#3

#2

C

#7

#6

#9

#10

#8

Bias Sequence Diagram

Begin by stitching a continuous strip of bias around the edges indicated by dark lines. Start at the open circle, follow the directional arrows, and stop at the closed circle. Stitch inside edge only. Add rest of bias. Tuck in raw edges. Finish stitching outside edges. See page 20 for details.

#7

#10

#9

#8

#6

#2L

#1L

Primroses

#3

#4

#2L

#12

#5

#2

#6

#10

#1

#9

#11

#12

#9

#8

#10

#7

#11

#8

#12

#7

#1L

58

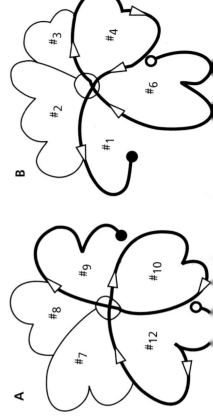

A

B

Bias Sequence Diagram

Begin by stitching a continuous strip of bias around the edges indicated by dark lines. Start at the open circle, follow the directional arrows, and stop at the closed circle. Stitch inside edge only. Add rest of bias. Tuck in raw edges. Finish stitching outside edges. See page 20 for details.

#3L

#4L

#2L

#5L

#1L

#6L

The Rose

#9L

#11

#12

#8L

#14

#16

#13

#15

#10

#7L

#9

#5L

#4L

Bias Sequence Diagram

Begin by stitching a continuous strip of bias around the edges indicated by dark lines. Start at the open circle, follow the directional arrows, and stop at the closed circle. Stitch inside edge only. Add rest of bias. Tuck in raw edges. Finish stitching outside edges. See page 20 for details.

Sweetpea

#4L

#5L

#6

#8

#9

#10

#3

#4

#5

#3

#4

#2

#3

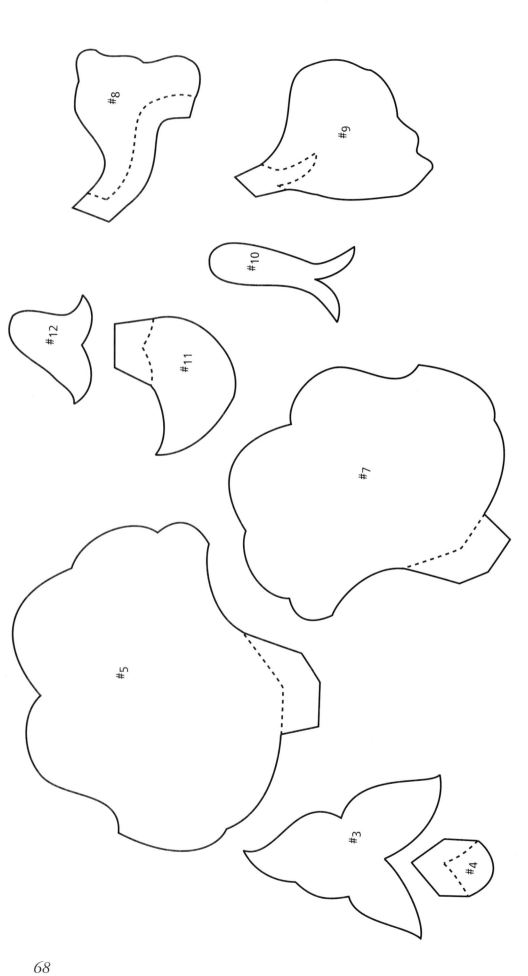

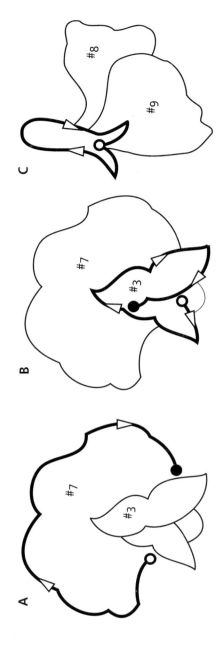

Bias Sequence Diagram

Begin by stitching a continuous strip of bias around the edges indicated by dark lines. Start at the open circle, follow the directional arrows, and stop at the closed circle. Stitch inside edge only. Add rest of bias. Tuck in raw edges. Finish stitching outside edges. See page 20 for details.

#4L

#5L

#2L

#1L

#3L

#6

#2

#1

Tulips

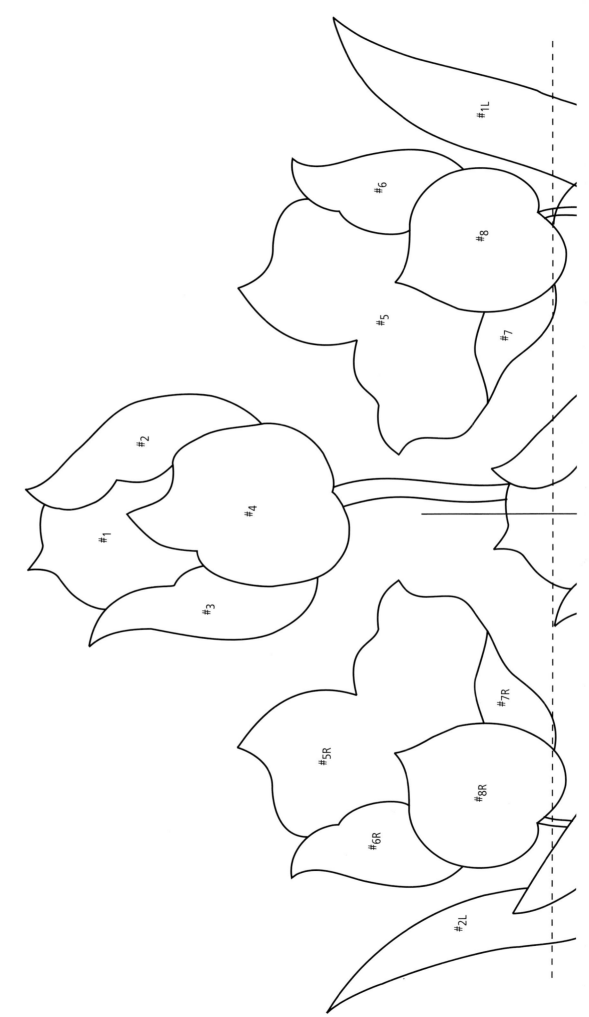

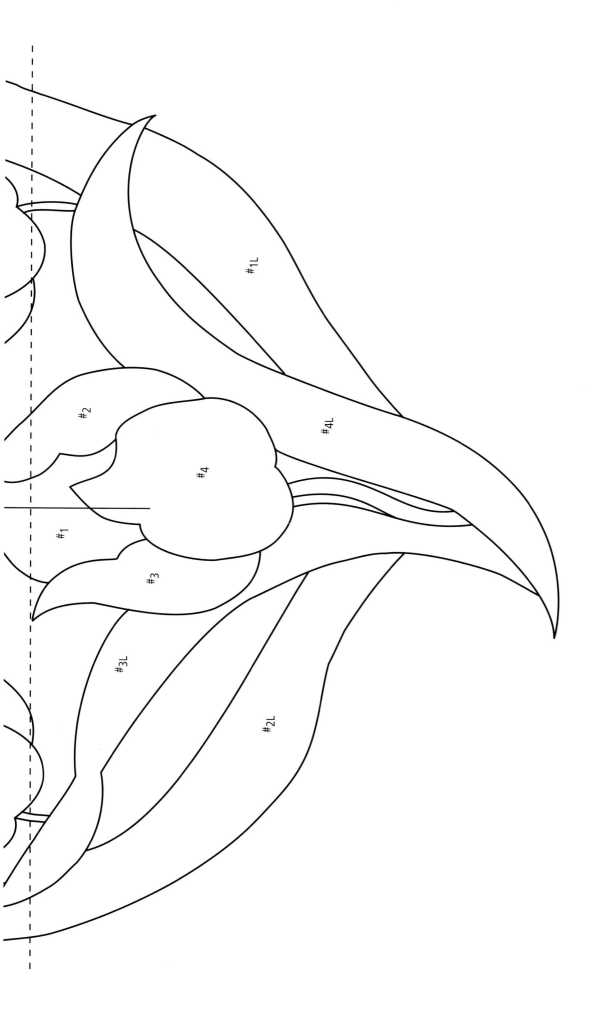

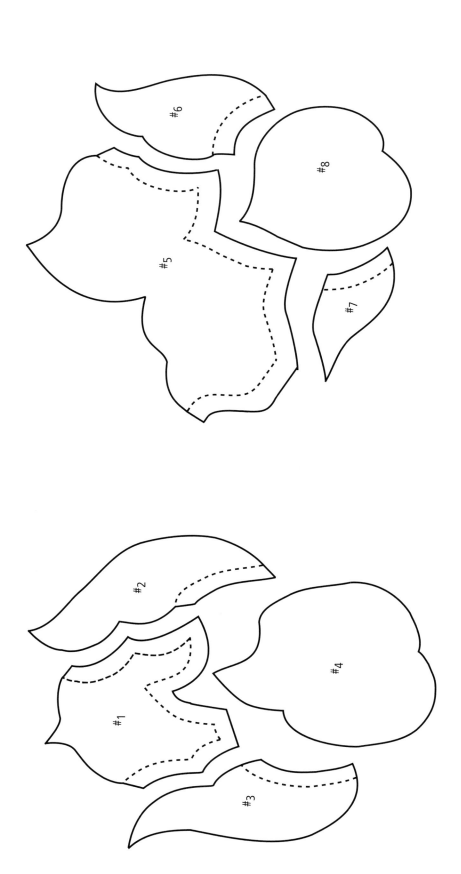

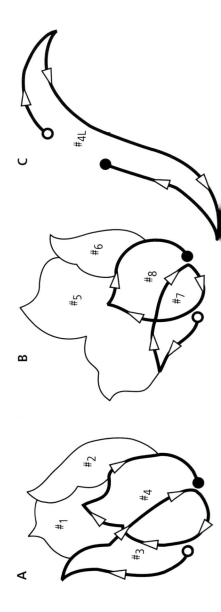

Bias Sequence Diagram

Begin by stitching a continuous strip of bias around the edges indicated by dark lines. Start at the open circle, follow the directional arrows, and stop at the closed circle. Stitch inside edge only. Add rest of bias. Tuck in raw edges. Finish stitching outside edges. See page 20 for details.

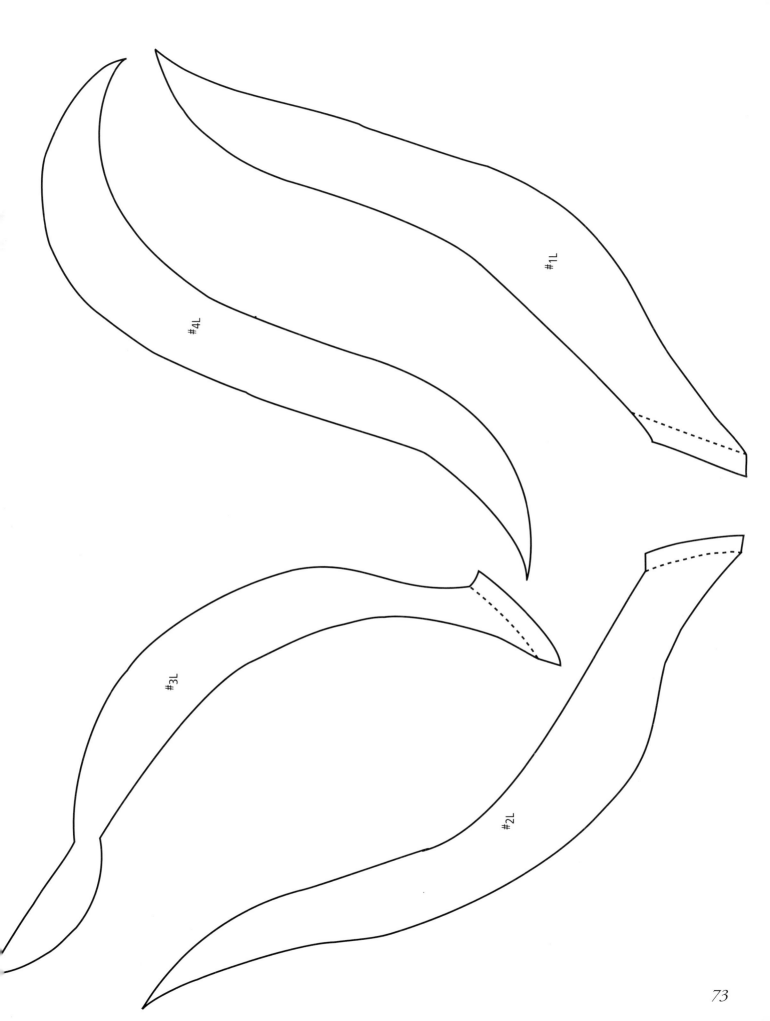

#1L

#4L

#3L

#2L

Waterlily

#14

#13

#15

#12

#16

Bias Sequence Diagram

Begin by stitching a continuous strip of bias around the edges indicated by dark lines. Start at the open circle, follow the directional arrows, and stop at the closed circle. Stitch inside edge only. Add rest of bias. Tuck in raw edges. Finish stitching outside edges. See page 20 for details.

76

Bibliography

1. Redoute, Pierre J. *The Most Beautiful Flowers*, Wellfleet Press, nd (ISBN: 1-55521-254-0)
2. Sienkiewicz, Elly. *Baltimore Beauties and Beyond, Studies in Classic Album Quilt Applique*, Vol. 1, C&T Publishing, Lafayette, CA (c1989).
3. Sienkiewicz, Elly. *Baltimore Beauties and Beyond, Studies in Classic Album Quilt Applique*. Vol. 2, C&T Publishing, Lafayette, CA (c1991).
4. Sienkiewicz, Elly. *Dimensional Applique, Baskets, Blooms and Baltimore Borders; A Pattern Companion to Vol. 2 of Baltimore Beauties and Beyond, Studies in Classic Album Quilt Applique*, C&T Publishing, Lafayette, CA (c1993).
5. Pearson, Nancy A. *Floral Appliques; Original Designs and Techniques for Medallion Quilts*, Quilt House Publishing, Saddle Brook, NJ (c1994). (ISBN: 1-881588-11-4).
6. Reinstatler, Laura M. *Botanical Wreaths; Nature's Glory in Applique*. That Patchwork Place, Inc., Bothell, WA (c1994). (ISBN: 1-56477-056-7).
7. Kimball, Jeana. *Red and Green; An Applique Tradition*, That Patchwork Place, Inc., Bothell, WA (c1990). (ISBN: 0-943574-68-4).
8. Wiechec, Philomena. *Celtic Quilt Designs*, Celtic Design Co., Sunnyvale, CA (c1980).
9. Leone, Diana. *Attic Windows; A Contemporary View*, Leone Publications, Mountain View, CA (c1988). (ISBN: 0-942786-09-2).
10. Beyers, Jenny. *Color Confidence for Quilters*, Quilt Digest Press, Gualala, CA (c1992). (ISBN: 0-913327-39-5).
11. Leone, Diana. *The New Sampler Quilt*, Leone Publications, Mountain View, CA (c1994).
12. Leone, Diana. *Fine Hand Quilting*, Leone Publications, Los Altos, CA (c1986).
13. Sienkiewicz, Elly. *Applique, 12 Easy Ways*, C&T Publishing, Lafayette, CA (c1991).
14. Martin, Judy and McCloskey, Marsha. *Pieced Borders, The Complete Resource*, Crosley-Griffith Publishing Co., Inc., Grunnell, IA (c1994).

QUILTING PERIODICALS:

American Quilter, American Quilter's Society, P.O. Box 3290, Paducha, KY 42002-9949.
Lady's Circle Patchwork Quilts, P.O. Box 516, Mount Morris, IL 61054-7972.
Quilt, Harris Publications, 1115 Broadway, New York, NY 10160-0261.
Quilter's Newsletter Magazine, Leman Publications, Box 4101, Golden, CO 80402-4101.
Quilting Today, P.O. Box 1736, Riverton, NJ 08077-9736.
Quilt World, P.O. Box 11304, Des Moines, IA 50347-1304.
Traditional Quiltworks, P.O. Box 1737, Riverton, NJ 08077-9736.

SOURCES

Start at your local quilt shop. If, after checking there you find you are still searching for that special piece of fabric or a particular tool, this brief list of sources may help:

Sonya Lee Barrington, 837 47th Avenue, SanFrancisco, CA 94121. Tie-dyes and marbelized fabrics.

Celtic Design Company, P.O. Box 2643, Sunnyvale, CA 94087. Metal Bias Bars (1/8" 3/16" 1/4" 3/8" 1/2" 5/8" and 3/4") books, patterns, and stencils.

Clotilde, Inc., 1909 S.W. First Avenue, Fort Lauderdale, FL 33315-2100. Serving all the Quilters needs by mail. You will find John James Sharps needles as well as a large variety of books and other notions.

Island Fibers, Rt. 1, Box 104, Washington Island, WI 54246. Wonderful hand-dyed cotton and silk fabrics by Kathy Sorensen.

Nancy's Notions, Ltd. 333 Beichl Avenue, P.O. Box 683 Beaver Dam, WI 53916-0683. Serving all the Quilters needs by mail, with a large variety of notions, books, and Celtic bias bars.

Quilting Creations by D.J. Inc., Box 508 Zoar, OH 44697 Serving Quilt Shops throughout the world with over three thousand stencils to choose from, including Celtic stencils.

Shades Inc., 585 Cobb Parkway S. Nunn Complex, Studio O, Marietta, GA 30062. Lots of wonderful hand-dyed and tie-dyed cotton and silk fabrics.

Skydyes, 83 Richmond Lane, West Hartford, CT 06117. Hand-painted cottons and silks for Quiltmakers and other Fiber Artists.

Acknowledgements

Teaching and lecturing about Celtic design has enabled me to visit so many interesting and lovely places and meet with Quilters throughout the United States, Canada, Europe, Australia, Ireland, and the rest of the British Isles. My sincerest appreciation to all of my students and followers who bought the earlier books on interlace and spirals. It is you who inspired me to develop the Celtic flowers, and it is to you that this book is dedicated.

I must also thank my friends, Audrey MacDougall, for showing me Scotland through a quilter's eyes and for sending me photographs of Benmore Gardens: and Bertha Boyes, for the Hibiscus design; and, of course, my sewing circle, Katherine Mooring, Isabelle Long, and Marmie Schraub (who continues to share her time and talents with me so willingly) These women have given me tremendous support and encouragement.

A big thank you to students Pat Peters, Rosella Keller, and Rosemary Kurtz for allowing me to include photographs of their work in the book; and again to Rosemary, who did such a beautiful quilting job on the *Through the Garden Gate* quilt.

A special thank you to my friend, Elizabeth Feinler, for the countless hours she spent with me editing the book, and my nephew, Colm Sweetman, for his talented design skills. They have both stood by and supported me throughout the project.

My grateful thanks to Hau Thi Long and Seamus O'Connor for their help and support over the years.

I would also like to applaud the many unique quilt shops throughout the world that carry my books, stencils, and bias bars. They do a wonderful job of retailing the fabrics and tools of our trade, and of furthering the art of quilting. I hope you will visit them often. They are exciting places to shop.